THREE MEN IN A BOAT

A Comedy of Errors (with Music)

by Blake Heathcote

Testaments Press

TESTAMENTS
PRESS

COPYRIGHT

TESTAMENTS
PRESS

CHARACTERS

in order of appearance

Jerome
Harris
George
Montmorency

Mrs. Poppet
Cabby
Woman with Baby
American Man
Barmaid
Herr Schlossen Bossen
Washerwoman
Cat
Old Man on the River
Woman Fishing
Man Fishing
Waiter
Woman in the Rain

PRODUCTION NOTES

Three Men in a Boat was written as a robust theatrical comedy, not a polite period piece. In its day, the novel was the original 'road trip' and 'buddy comedy,' and was slammed by critics for what they saw as a celebration of Low Life – which didn't stop it from from being an instant success and selling hundreds of thousands of copies in England alone, and over a million in the United States.

These are three young men on a vacation, looking to blow off some steam, drink too much, and hopefully meet more than a few girls. They are middle-class clerks who live in a very proper Victorian world, but while on holiday do what they can to try to break free of the constraints of their working worlds. That sense of repressed enthusiasm and energy is key to the performances, and is what keeps the play bristling with life. Imagine a young John Cleese as the character Harris, and you begin to get a sense of the spirit of the production at its best.

ACTORS & DOUBLING

The play is written for five actors: four men, and one woman. The actors playing the three men perform only their parts throughout, with one exception. The actor playing "Jerome" reads a few lines as Jerome's dog, Montmorency. Montmorency is never seen (apart from a few lines read by the actor playing Jerome); the actors should react to Montmorency as though he was very much there with them throughout. It's especially important for Jerome to establish and remind us of the presence of Montmorency throughout. The 'swing' actors, Woman and Man, each play multiple roles.

SETS

The script's scene divisions are typically used to show short passages of time. The play is intended to move very swiftly and with a very light touch. This is dependent on agile direction and production design, which will allow the scenes to flow fluidly from one to the next using a minimum of scenery. There is a great deal of the energy and spark of the 'Music Hall' in the play: take this as a cue and run with it!

For the various settings – and there are many – I encourage the use of whatever will suggest location using a minimum of elements. (There are some example photographs in the Appendix.) Lighting can be very effective in this regard, especially in such scenes as Hampton Court Maze or the Alhambra Supper Club.

The Author hopes that the eponymous "boat" will not bog down the production. Ideally, it will be a large, flexible, and imaginative prop that the actors can inhabit, as well as comfortably manoeuvre and interact with.

LIGHTING

With minimal scenery, lighting will be essential to suggest different parts of the river, shifting times of day, and most challengingly, the labyrinth of Hampton Court Maze.

MUSIC

Music is used throughout to help establish the mood of the various scenes through underscoring and accompaniment. This has been done using live music (keyboard), as well as pre-recorded music.

The Music Hall song, "Put on Your Ta Ta, Little Girlie," is performed somewhat raggedly at the top of Act One; but when it is reprised at the play's end in Act Two, it should be crisp, bright, and performed with great energy and enthusiasm, very much in contrast to Act One.

There are additional production details and photographs on the play's webpage: www.blakeheathcote.com/three-men.html

ACT ONE

Scene 1

Jerome enters an empty stage and talks to the audience. He carries a manuscript under his arm, to which he refers as he talks.

Jerome *(out)*: The chief beauty of this story lies not so much in the usefulness of the information it conveys, but in its *truth*-fulness. These are the brief chronicles of events that really happened. All I've done is to add a bit of colour and seasoning, and for that no extra charge has been added. There were four of us. George…

George enters upstage tentatively.

Jerome *(out)*: William Samuel Harris…

Harris also enters tentatively and waits near George.

Jerome *(out)*: And myself.

Jerome does a quick count on his fingers. SFX a bark offstage.

Jerome *(out)*: Oh, and Montmorency, my dog. Here, boy!

He welcomes and pats the [unseen] dog.

Harris *(sotto voce):* Just tell the story and leave the dog alone…

1

Jerome *(out)*:   While other stories may be more eventful or more philosophical, none is as hopelessly or incurably truthful as this one. George, Harris, and Montmorency are not poetic ideals, but things of flesh and blood. Particularly Harris, who weighs in at nearly 13 stone.

Harris *(to George)*:   What's he saying?

Jerome *(out)*:   The story of "Three Men in a Boat."

> *Music begins: the intro to "Put On Your Tat-Tas Little Girlie."*

Jerome *(out)*:   It was the summer of 1889. A blissful time to be young and single and on the prowl for girls. The three of us met auditioning for our club's annual amateur theatrical extravaganza.

> *An oversized cloth drop unfurls directly behind George and Harris, startling them. The drop advertises a men's club, The Alhambra, much in the style of an old music hall playbill, which momentarily distracts George and Harris. George then nudges Harris into action, and they begin attempting to perform a dance routine to the piano music that has been vamping underneath.*

Jerome *(out)*:   The Club's a wonderful place: cozy and plenty of opportunity to corrupt yourself. Every year we'd lace up our boots and do our level best to win a featured spot in the show.

> *George and Harris are beginning to lose what little synchronization to which they were aspiring in their dance routine, and begin to snap at one another.*

Jerome *(out)*:   Harris is the tall one with the size twenty-seven shoes. Too overbearing for leading man material.

Whereas George is no-one's enemy, and we all know how tedious that is. They probably would have chosen me if I hadn't pulled a fetlock on the day of the auditions.

> *Jerome nurses his leg. George and Harris have lumbered to a stop and attempt to start again as the music continues under.*

Jerome (*out*): So instead of leading men, we were shoved to the back of the chorus and became the very best of friends.

Harris: Are you doing this or not, fathead?!

> *Harris glowers at Jerome, and then marks his steps that much harder in an attempt to force the routine into sync. Jerome steps back into line and they finish the number in a somewhat ragged fashion as the music ends.*
>
> *They congratulate one another as the Alhambra drop is removed and the lights cross-fade for a scene change.*

Scene 2

> *As the scene changes to Jerome's sitting room. George and Harris exit to bring on chairs and drinks, and Jerome comes forward and talks to the audience.*

Jerome (*out*): After the performances – actually, during most of the performances as well – we liked to relax with a drink or two.

> *George and Harris enter with chairs, make themselves comfortable, and leave Jerome's chair*

with his drink on it.

Jerome *(out)*: We discussed the world and all that was wrong with it, and how bad we were. From a medical point of view, I mean. We all felt pretty seedy.

Harris: Let's be frank. Medically speaking, we are not the men we were.

George: I know I'm not.

Jerome: Nerves, I think.

Harris: The hurly burly of modern life.

George: I'd put even money on my spleen being the culprit.

> *George explores his midsection like a nearsighted man searching for loose change on a sandy beach.*

Harris: Where *is* the spleen?

George: Not a clue.

Jerome: Isn't that the one that looks like Albania?

Harris: What does your doctor say?

George: He says his patients tell him the most appalling things and then they show them to him. So I don't ask anymore.

Jerome: With me, it's my liver.

Harris: What is?

Jerome: That's out of whack.

George: At times it feels like an elf is swimming in my brain.

Harris: Shut up, George. *(to Jerome)* Why your liver?

Jerome pulls a leaflet out of a pocket.

Jerome: I've been reading a pamphlet for these little liver pills, and as it happens I have all the symptoms. The worst being, "...a general disinclination to work of any kind." That feeling never leaves me for a day, which I think says something.

Harris: When I was a boy, my Uncle Terry used to clump me across the side of the head when he wanted something done. "You skulking little devil," he'd bark, "Get up and do something for your living!" None of your little pills or Albanias. Funny thing was, it used to work.

He rises to refresh his drink.

George: Medical science was far less advanced in those days.

Jerome: Old-fashioned remedies are sometimes the best. *(He drinks)*

George: Regardless, I think it's safe to say that none of us are truly healthy. I mean I've all but lost my appetite.

Jerome: And me.

Harris: Couldn't even think of food.

> *With a knock, Mrs. Poppet, Jerome's landlady, enters carrying a tray laden with food. The boys stand.*

Mrs. Poppet: Here you are, Gentlemen. A little late but better than never.

> *Various ad-libbed "ahhhs" and "wonderfuls" and other such sounds of appreciation as they rally*

round the table laden with the food.

Jerome: Thank you Mrs. Poppet.

Mrs. Poppet: Homemade, that is. Give you boys something to tuck into.

She bustles out and they tuck into the food.

George: Lovely.

Jerome and Harris murmur agreement as they eat.

The lights fade.

Scene 3

Jerome's flat about an hour later. As the lights restore, the men are discovered relaxing in various states of digestive contentment.

Jerome: We'd best face it: modern life has taken its toll.

George: With knobs on.

Harris: My grandfather never had a sick day in his life. Now look at me: a near invalid.

George offers Jerome the cheese plate.

George: Last bit of cheese, J?

Jerome: I couldn't. Well. All right.

He takes the cheese.

Harris: And you know what the cause is?

George *(belches):* Work…?

Harris: Over-work.

Jerome: Overwork. Absolutely.

Harris: What we need is complete rest.

George: And a change. *(belches)*

Harris: It's the strain on our brains that's caused the overload. If we only had a break from it all. Some kind of a holiday…

George: — An expedition —

Jerome: Far from the madding crowd. Some half-forgotten nook hidden away from civilization.

Harris: Sounds like the sort of place where everyone goes to bed at eight o'clock and you have to walk ten miles to get a drink. All yoghurt and no ashtrays.

George: Something out of doors to fortify us and restore our appetites.

Harris: Why not an ocean cruise? Can't beat salt water for clearing your sinuses.

Jerome: Well, that's fine for our sinuses, but we'll smell like dead Sea Bass for a month and the trip will be a fading memory long before we get over being seasick.

George: Why don't we rent a boat and row up the river? We'll have fresh air, exercise, and quiet, and the hard work will make us sleep like infants.

Harris: If you slept any more, George, you might as well be dead and save money on bed and board.

Jerome: He has a point, George.

George: But what do you think? Boating all day, tenting it at night?

Jerome: It suits me. Harris?

Harris: As long as I don't end up doing all the work as usual.

George: Harris, get a map. George, you fetch the sporting goods catalogue.

> *George and Harris exit to fetch these. Jerome talks to the audience.*

Jerome (*out*): And so we discussed plans. George and I were in favour of camping, while Harris wanted to stay at Inns, as he knew several along the river where we could get a drop of the finest Scotch whisky we'd ever tasted. Harris always knows a place 'round the corner where you can get something brilliant in the drinking line. But we stood firm on sleeping outdoors.

> *Harris and George have returned. Harris spreads out a map on the floor while George thumbs through a sporting goods catalogue.*

Harris: I don't know about this camping business...

George: Harris! Sleeping under the stars!

Jerome: At one with the grand old river and all her history.

> *Music underscores as Jerome paints a picture.*

Jerome: Slowly the memory of the sun fades from the hearts of the cold, sad clouds. We run the little boat into some quiet inlet, the tent is pitched and the simple supper cooked and eaten. And while we sit there, the moon stoops down to kiss the water and throws her silver arms around it as we fall asleep beneath the great still stars, and dream that the world is young again: the simple, stately home where mankind was born so many thousands of years before.

Music ends.

Harris: How about when it rains?

Jerome: There is no poetry about you. No yearning for the unattainable.

Harris: I certainly hope not.

Jerome *(to George):* If his eyes fill with tears, you can bet he's been eating onions.

Harris *(to George):* What's he yammering on about?

Jerome: I'm talking about communing with nature before someone slaps a fence around it and start charging admission! Seeing the world as it was meant to be seen!

Harris: And I'm talking about it pouring rain and being soaked to the skin and everything from the bread to our underdrawers is rank with mildew.

George: I see what you mean...

Jerome: George...!

George: The tent is soaking wet and it weighs a ton and fights you every inch of the way when you try to get it up —

Harris: — and the tobacco's damp and the jam is damp and the salt is damp and the tent's getting worse —

George: — and J, you know how hopeless you are with the simplest of tasks in the best of circumstances.

Jerome: But it's a chance to really get to know one another!

Harris: If have to know much more about either one of you, I'm going to need a drink and a warm bed. Inns and guest houses, that's the answer.

Jerome: Expensive.

> *They all murmur concern. There is a reflective silence as they consider the options. Then George finds inspiration in his catalogue, and holds it up to illustrate.*

George: We could rent a boat with a canvas cover!

> *SFX Montmorency barks in complaint. Jerome comforts him.*

Harris: A what?

> *He references an example in his catalogue.*

George: You stick these hoops on your boat, stretch a tent over the top, then fasten it all round. It looks very cozy.

Harris: — Like a floating casket —

George: It can't be half as hard to put up as a regular tent. And we can sleep in town if the weather turns bad.

Jerome: Now that's an interesting idea…

Harris: Beginner's luck.

George: It'd be the best of both worlds.

Jerome: Harris?

Beat.

Harris: Oh, all right.

Jerome *(to Harris):* Get some paper and a pencil and make a list. And George, you go through the catalogue and call off what we need.

> *George picks up the catalogue as Harris exits in search of some paper and a pencil.*

Harris: But I'm bringing a bottle of whisky in case we get upset.

Jerome *(out):* Harris harped too much on getting upset. It was the wrong spirit for the trip. *(beat)* But I'm glad we brought the whisky. *(to George)* Right. Now, what's needed?

George *(reading):* There's a terrific pair of hip waders here. I've always wanted to try those —

> *Harris returns with paper and pencil. He makes notes throughout the following.*

Harris: We'll need some meat. Beef —

Jerome: — pork —

> *George contributes without looking up from his catalogue.*

George: — lamb —

Harris: — smoked fish —

Jerome: — chicken —

George *(reading):* — mountaineering cleats —

Jerome: — spicy sausage. Polish —

Harris: — spicy and plain —

Jerome — meat pies.

George: Steak. No. Kidney. No. Um —

Jerome: I have this sticky concoction you mix with water and turns into something called 'lemonade.'

George: — That sounds appalling —

Harris (*writing furiously*): Just a minute, just a minute! Bread, butter, tea, sugar, milk, lemon-something —

Jerome: — tobacco, beer, salt, tinned fruit, fresh fruit —

George: — vegetables —

Jerome: — swedes, beetroot, persimmons, kumquats —

Harris: I am not writing down anything I can't spell!

Jerome: — potatoes, cake, biscuits —

George: — plates, knives, forks, cups —

Harris: Hold on, hold on…!

Harris's pencil is giving him trouble.

George: — mugs, tea pot, napkins, hamper…

Harris: What kind of pencil do you call this?!

George (*with catalogue*): There's nothing like a catalogue to remind you of things you didn't know you needed.

Harris struggles with the pencil.

Jerome: What about a stove?

> *Harris hurls away the offending pencil.*

George *(head in catalogue)*: Stove... stove...

> *He goes searching for a stove in the catalogue.*

Jerome: One of those camping things with the whatsit.

Harris *(stressed)*: I need more paper...

> *Harris holds up his list to illustrate as George looks up from his catalogue.*

George: You know, we're on the wrong track altogether. We shouldn't think of the things we could do with, but only the things we can't do without.

> *In a silent fury, Harris slowly and methodically tears up his list while George continues to browse.*

George: Now let me see...

Jerome *(out)*: George comes out quite sensible at times. I call that downright wisdom. Not just for the trip up the river, but for our journey in life as well. How many people, on this voyage, load up the boat 'till it is ever in danger of being swamped with a mountain of foolish things which they think essential to the pleasure and comfort of the trip, only to discover...

> *Harris has walked up behind Jerome with his hands full of the shredded shopping list, which he showers over Jerome's head, prompting Jerome to stop talking. Harris sits. George closes the catalogue and looks up thoughtfully.*

George: How 'bout this: we take a blanket, one lamp, one bar of soap, one toothbrush —

Harris: — I'm not using your ruddy toothbrush!

Jerome: We'll take one each. What else, George?

George: Shaving tackle and big towels for having a swim first thing in the morning. We'll only need one change of clothes.

Harris: One...?

George: We'll just give things a wash in the river as we go.

Jerome: Have you done that before?

George: Oh, absolutely...

He nods his head perhaps too much in the affirmative.

Jerome *(out)*: We discovered, in the days to come, that George was a miserable liar—

George: — hundreds of times —

Jerome *(out)*: — who knew nothing whatsoever about washing clothes. But I anticipate.

Harris: Can we please get back to the food? Now as I see it, we'll have eggs, bacon, cold meat, bread, butter, and jam for breakfast. Then cold meat, bread, butter, and jam for lunch. And the same for dinner. There. That was easy.

Satisfied, he folds himself into a chair.

George: We'll need a frying pan.

Harris: Too indigestible.

He laughs merrily; the others do not.

Jerome: That's a lot of bread and jam.

Harris: All right, all right. We'll get some cheese. One of those big round things that smells like liniment.

Jerome: Good.

Harris: Right.

George: No.

Harris: What?

George: No cheese.

Harris: What do you mean "No Cheese?"

George: The smell will take over the boat.

Harris: Stop talking drivel, George. We'll have enough of that on the trip.

George: No, hear me out.

Music.

George: I met a friend on holiday once who bought a couple of large rounds of ripe Stilton with a 200 horsepower smell that carried three miles and could knock a man flat at a hundred yards. He asked me to take them back home for him on the train. The train was crowded, but I managed to squeeze in. Then one by one the people in the compartment fell back from the smell. A fat woman next to me began to fidget and finally escaped to catch her breath in a cattle car. A solemn looking man – he worked in the sewers, I think – said it reminded him of a musk ox in heat, and then he and three others hurt themselves trying to get out of the compartment at the same time. I reached the station more or less intact and took the cheeses to my friend's house. But his wife, tears streaming down her face and a handkerchief over her nose, threatened to call the police and divorce him if I left the them with her. So I hauled them to the city dump. But the workmen complained that the smell made them dizzy and faint. I finally had to take them to a seaside town and bury them on the beach. It gained the place quite a reputation. Visitors said they had never noticed before how strong the air was, and people with asthma and bronchitis used to throng there for years afterwards to take the air and cleanse their lungs.

Beat.

Harris: Right. Forget the cheese.

Jerome: Why don't we each take charge of one thing. Harris, you do food and maps, George'll organize the equipment and the boat, and I'll take care of utensils and other essentials. We'll pack our own kits and convene back here Friday evening to organize.

Harris: Fine.

George: I have to work Saturday until two, so I'll meet you up river after that.

Jerome: Then a toast to three men and their boat, and their search for their —

Harris: — Yes, yes, yes, yes, yes… Fine, cheers.

All: Cheers!

Music begins under as they raise their glasses in a toast, drain them, then exit briskly in various directions.

Scene 4

Jerome's flat, Friday evening. As the lights slowly crossfade then restore, Jerome, Harris, and George come and go, piling their respective items in the centre of the room. This goes on for a time. Finally they finish and sit down gazing at the mountain of stuff.

George: Quite a large pile.

Jerome: I kept mine to the minimum.

Harris: I know I did. What time do you have?

Jerome: 12.30.

Harris: Then I'm going to sleep.

> *He promptly settles himself down in an armchair.*

Jerome: Now what the devil did I do with my toothbrush…?

> *He starts to search through the mountain of luggage.*

George: I'll take the blue chair, J. Goodnight, chaps.

Jerome: Where in the name of… *(out)* My toothbrush haunts me when I travel. Makes my life a misery. I dream I haven't packed it, then wake up in a cold sweat and pack it before I've used it, and then have to unpack it again to use it in the morning. I had to turn every blesséd thing inside out looking for it, and finally found it inside my boot wrapped in a handkerchief.

> *Harris hurls something at J.*

Harris: Will you shut up! I'll wake us at six.

He pulls a blanket over his head.

Music as the lights fade to black.

Scene 5

The lights fade up to suggest morning. The men are asleep in a variety of positions and general disarray.

SFX clock chiming 9.

Jerome awakes sleepily, then registers the time.

Jerome: It's nine o'clock! Harris!

He hurls his blanket at Harris.

Jerome: Harris!

Harris: It's wha…?

Jerome: It's nine o'clock!

Harris: I thought you wanted to get up at six!

Jerome: I did! Why didn't you wake us?

Harris: Now we won't get on the water till after twelve. I wonder why you take the trouble to get up at all sometimes! Bleeding bloody —

He is tangled in his blanket. After a prolonged struggle, he manages to extricate himself.

Jerome: — You'd have lain there snoring the whole two weeks if I hadn't.

He exits. Harris wraps his blanket around
George's head, and then shouts.

Harris: George!

George lurches to consciousness and stumbles
blindly, unable to untangle himself.

George: Wassamatter...?

Harris: Get up you fatheaded chunk. It's quarter to ten!

George: What? I'm due at the bank in fifteen minutes! What
the devil...?

As George struggles to escape the tendrils of the
blanket, Jerome enters with a tray of tea and buns
and a newspaper, which he tosses at George.

Jerome: It's only nine, George. Harris made us sleep in. Read
us the weather.

George, now free, unfolds the paper and begins to
read.

Harris: The important thing is a really good breakfast.

Jerome: Too bad we packed the food.

Harris: No eggs?

Jerome: No.

George (*reading*): Been another boating fatality.

Harris: Bacon? Jam? Little buns with cream filling?

Jerome: Stale bread and tea.

George (*reading*): Whole family drowned.

Harris: Well. Milk and sugar for me.

Jerome: Both packed. Sorry.

> *He pours and hands out cups of tea. Harris accepts his with a heavy heart.*

George (*reading*): Washed out to sea without a trace.

Jerome: What's the weather?

George (*reading*): "Occasional local thunderstorms, east wind, and general depression over the area. Barometer falling."

Harris: Well, straight off, pay no attention to the forecast. They're probably speculating about conditions next spring. Who packed my razor?

George (*reading*): A ferry off the coast of Ireland sank with all hands.

> *Jerome considers the mountain of luggage.*

Jerome: There's a good deal of stuff here...

Harris: It looks like there's a lot. But once we load it in the boat, we'll be glad we packed so wisely. I'm using your razor, J.

> *He exits.*

George: I'd better run. See you up river around three.

> *He exits.*

Jerome *(out)*:   And with that, George disappeared, leaving the transportation of the provisions and the gear to Harris and me. Which meant to me alone. Travel's a funny thing. Endless headaches getting ready, then getting the things you've got ready down to where you have to go from, and then getting to the place itself, and then lugging the stuff around, and then getting it all back home again and trying to find the places that you dug it all out from in the first place to put it all back again. I decided to make the first bit easy and hired a cab.

> *During the above, a Cabby enters with a luggage truck.*

Cabby: Oi!

Jerome: Just these things here.

Cabby: I don't handle moving jobs.

Jerome: We're just going boating up river for a few days.

> *As the Cabby loads the truck through the following, Jerome does an inventory of the luggage.*

Cabby: Not going to starve, are you.

Jerome *(still counting)*:   We're bringing more than just food. There's books and writing materials —

Cabby: Don't forget them bookcases and arm chairs…

Jerome: — blankets and pillows and a folding table —

Cabby: Look, Squire, I'll charge you double if you makes me listen. What time's your train?

Jerome: 11.05.

Cabby: You got fifteen minutes. Best get your skates on.

> *Cabby exits with luggage.*

Jerome: Harris!

> *Jerome grabs his Gladstone and hat, as Harris enters with bits of toilet paper stuck all over his face having cut himself, and carrying a razor which he hurls away in a temper.*

Harris: You call that a razor? Look at me! Where are the things?

Jerome: On the way to the station. Come on. Montmorency!

> *Harris exits. There is a bark from Montmorency. Jerome talks to the audience.*

Jerome *(out)*:   And so we finally got to Kingston and our boat.

> *Jerome exits as we hear a train whistle and other railway SFX. The lights fade.*
>
> *Music.*

Scene 6

> *Lights come up revealling the eponymous boat, moored riverside at a spot on the Thames near Kingston. Jerome and Harris enter searching for it, Harris with his head buried in a map.*

Harris: We should be right around here somewhere.

Jerome: We are. We're right here.

Harris: Where's this boat then?

Jerome: The rental agent said it'd be tied up near the… what's that?

Harris: Driftwood.

Jerome *(reads)*: "The Pride of the Thames." *(He checks the paperwork)* This is it.

Harris: You're joking.

Jerome: I'm not.

Harris: I'm not getting in that. Do you mean to tell me this is what George arranged for us?

Jerome: It has a certain rustic appeal.

Harris: Rustic? Primitive, you mean! I was expecting a sort of compact yacht. Or at the very least some kind of glorified houseboat. But not this… this… this… this… this…

Jerome: He probably thought a smaller boat might fill the bill.

Harris: George? Think? When I see him, I'm going to beat him to death with what's left of that oar.

Jerome: That's a bit extreme.

Harris: Not a bit of it. And afterwards I'll dance on his grave.

Jerome: We're stuck with it now and it's already half past twelve. I suggest we make the best of it. We'll row up to meet George, and then you can dance on his grave.

Harris: Right.

Harris begins to hurl things into the boat.

Harris: But I'll tell you one thing for free, matey. We'll be hip-deep in snow in the dead of summer before I let him forget this one.

> *Music. Harris organizes the things in the boat as Jerome talks to the audience.*

Jerome *(out)*:   I tried to remind Harris that the point of the journey was rest and reflection —

Harris: We'll probably sink and end up a trifling news item on page five —

Jerome *(out)*:   — and that the other fellow was trying his best, regardless of the outcome —

Harris: — but there, we're loaded. You man the oars. I'll navigate.

Jerome: Not much room.

Harris *(acidly):* Then why don't you walk?

Jerome: No, no. It's very… bohemian. Suits my mood.

Harris: Then push off.

Jerome: Come on, boy.

> *Montmorency barks. Jerome scratches Monty's ears, then takes the oars. Harris stretches out with a guidebook. The lights crossfade.*

Scene 7

*As the lights restore, Jerome is rowing with
waning enthusiasm while Harris remains
stretched out as he reads the guidebook.*

Jerome: Coming up on Sanford Lock.

Harris *(reading)*: That's an excellent place to drown, it says
here. The undertow's very strong.

Looks at something a few yards distant.

Harris: What's that sign say?

Jerome *(reads)*: "Danger: two men drowned here last summer
while swimming."

Harris: Which presumably is why those boys are using it as a
diving board...

SFX water splash.

Harris: Checking to see if it's *actually* dangerous, or only if you
read signs.

SFX splash of water.

Harris: Now I've marked all the places in my guidebook
where I want to stop. Kingston, for example, was the
spot where Caesar crossed the river with his Roman
legions. *(to Jerome)* Did you know that? I thought
not. Good Queen Bess crossed the river there, too.
According to this, she stopped at pretty much every
inn and tavern in the neighbourhood. Apparently the
Virgin Queen was nuts on pubs. My kind of girl.

*As Jerome talks, Harris reads aloud from the
guidebook. The actor can improvise, or use text*

25

*suggested in the Appendix. He reads not so loud
as to understand what he is saying, but loud
enough to make clear that he is engrossed and
paying no attention whatsoever to Jerome.*

Jerome *(out)*: I wonder if Harris, turning over some improbable
new leaf, became a great and good man, got to be Prime
Minister, and died. Would they put up signs in pubs
he'd knocked a few back in? "Harris had a glass of beer
in this house"; or "Harris had two glasses of port in
the lounge during the summer of '88'; and "Harris was
tossed out of here in December '86."

*When Harris sees that Jerome has stopped
talking and is smiling at him, he stops his reading
abruptly.*

Harris: What are you grinning about? Put your back into it!

*Harris returns to his reading aloud as Jerome once
again talks to the audience.*

Jerome *(out)*: No, there'd be too many of them. It would only
be the places he'd never entered that would become
famous. "Only house in South London that Harris never
had a drink in." People would flock to see what could
have been the matter with it.

*As Jerome finishes, Harris lays down his guide
and reflects on a sentimental memory.*

Harris: I had an uncle in Kingston whose house used to be
the mansion of some great panjandrum or something. It
had a huge hand-carved oak staircase and this massive
room where we used to play cricket indoors when it
rained. Oak panelling, floor to ceiling.

Jerome: Must have been beautiful.

Harris: It was appalling, like living in a church. But he covered up all the oak with blue wallpaper, and made it very bright and cheery.

Jerome: You're not serious...!

Harris: J, old sock, everyone has something he doesn't want, while others have something else he'd sell his mother to white slavers for. Sickly bed-ridden students yearn to study, while I could never catch so much as a stiff neck during final exams. Funny thing, life.

Jerome: We are but as grass that withers and is cut down.

Harris: You said it. (*He yawns and stretches*) Might as well put my boating togs on.

> *Music.*
>
> *Jerome stops rowing and talks to the audience. Harris digs into his belongings and pulls out his jacket – which boasts an extremely vivid fabric.*

Jerome (*out*): It was wonderful to be on the river. There was a brilliant tangle of bright blazers, multi-coloured parasols, rugs and cloaks and streaming ribbons, all bound together, like a huge box of flowers, every hue and shade, thrown pell-mell in a rainbow heap on the glistening surface of the river...

> *Jerome regards Harris's jacket.*

Jerome (*out*): And still, Harris – in that jacket – stood out like an angry boil on the end of a fat man's nose.

Harris: What do you think? Adds a splash of colour to the old river.

Jerome: And then some.

Harris: I think it brings out my hair.

Jerome: Yes, probably bring it out in clumps.

Harris: J, the less taste someone has in clothing, the more stubborn he is about it. Can't you see that?

Jerome: I can't see anything; your jacket's blinding me. What colour *is* that?

Harris: They didn't have a name for it.

Jerome: I can think of one or two.

Harris: It may be daring, but compared to what George bought...

Jerome: Worse than that?

Harris: Like an explosion in a paint factory. We can use him as a beacon at night.

Jerome: Maybe it'll keep the bats and crows away.

Harris: As long as it doesn't scare off girls.

Jerome: We're bound to meet one or two who won't run screaming.

George *(off)*: Hey!!

Harris *(looks)*: What's that?

SFX Montmorency barks through he following

Jerome *(looks)*: I think someone's clothes have caught fire...!

George *(off)*: Hallo...!!

Harris: Those aren't flames, that's George's jacket! Hallo!

SFX Montmorency barking.

Jerome: It's cured Monty of his colour-blindness.

Harris *(waving):* George!

SFX Montmorency barks and Jerome calms him.

George *(off):* Meet you by the bank!!

They negotiate the boat to the shore.

George enters carrying an oddly shaped package wrapped in paper, round at one end with a long handle. He wears an extremely colourful jacket.

Jerome *(out):* And so we rendezvoused with George and his blazer.

Jerome and Harris disembark.

George: Hallo!

Harris: Have a nice sleep at the bank?

George: Yes, thanks. Looking forward to stretching out and relaxing a bit.

He sees the boat.

George: It's much bigger than I expected…!

Harris: Bigger!?

George: Where should I put my things?

Harris *(menacingly):* Let *me* show him.

Jerome: We'd better repack or we'll sink like a rock.

> *Harris and Jerome begin hauling things out of the boat and rearranging. George ignores this and begins to unwrap his mystery package, and catches Harris's attention.*

Jerome: What's that? We've got a frying pan.

George: They're all the rage this year. It's a banjo!

> *SFX banjo twang.*

Harris *(not pleased):* You don't play the banjo.

George: Not yet, but I have an instruction book. The sales clerk assured me it's very easy.

Harris: Bound to be a sure thing, then.

Jerome: George, lend a hand here. It's been a long day.

> *Harris and Jerome rearrange luggage to accommodate George. George, deaf to the request for help, sits in the bow and begins to plunk and strum his banjo. Montmorency howls. George stops and glowers at Monty. Montmorency stops. George plays. Montmorency howls.*

George: What's he want to howl like that for when I'm playing?

Harris: What do you want to play like that for when he's howling? He's got a musical ear and your playing makes him howl.

> *Montmorency howls as George continues to plunk and strum awkwardly. Harris continues rearranging the luggage grimly while Jerome talks to the audience.*

Jerome *(out)*:   George is sensitive about his music. He took up
the bagpipes once, but his landlady complained that the
pregnant woman on the next floor was afraid the sound
would damage her child. So he practiced in the park
at night, but people reported him to the police saying
they'd heard the horrific shrieks of a murder and the
dying gurgles of the victim. Vigilantes hunted George
down and captured him, and he lost heart after that.

> *George has continued to plunk through this.*
> *Harris has finally had his fill and grabs the banjo.*

Harris: Right. That's it!

George: Hey!

Harris: J and I want to admire it while you're rowing us up
river. You look sufficiently refreshed, so grab the oars.

> *George reluctantly settles in and begins to row*
> *while Harris and Jerome recline and relax.*

Harris: That's it, full deep strokes. So you see, J, there is some
poetry to life after all.

> *Music. Lights fade to black.*

Scene 8

The lights come up.

Time has passed. George still labours at the oars,
while Jerome reads the guidebook and Harris
scans the horizon.

Jerome: Where are we?

Harris: Hampton Court coming up.

George: Have you ever been to the maze here? Shrubs 12 feet high. You can wander around lost for hours.

Jerome: Sounds like a laugh riot.

Harris: I went in once to show somebody the way. Studied the map; complete waste of time. Dead simple.

George: I'd like to have a look.

Harris: I've just finished telling you what a waste of time it is.

> *He snaps the guidebook shut and tosses it to Jerome.*

Jerome: Just for ten minutes. Come on, boy.

> *Montmorency barks. They exit the boat and move it off as the lights crossfade.*

Scene 9

> *The scene changes to the Hampton Court Maze. A bench is brought onstage as a part of the Maze.*
>
> *The men re-enter a moment later. The Maze remains largely unseen, leaving it to the actors and lighting to suggest a kind of baffling natural puzzle. Perhaps some abstract set elements could be moved on to help define the Maze's passages.*

Jerome *(nose in book)*: It's fascinating about Henry VIII and this place. Do you know the history behind Hampton Court?

Harris: No.

Jerome: Would you like to?

Harris: I'd rather have needles stuck in my eyes.

George: Here's the entrance.

Harris: We'll go in so that you can say you've been, but it's absurd to even call it a maze. You simply keep taking the first turn to the right. We'll walk round for ten minutes, and then get some lunch.

> *Music underscores throughout. They enter the 'Maze' and begin their journey. Their meandering journey should suit the theatre – it might be around the stage, or through and around the audience. They are never able to 'see' more than a couple of feet ahead because of the maze. Lighting could be used to great effect here. There should be several 'comings and goings', in whatever way best suits the space.*

George: Are you sure this is the right way?

Harris: Mazes have the same logic as a span bridge or a tea kettle, George. What you have to learn is patience.

> *He trips on something unseen and curses, which brings him face to face with an American Man who has wandered into the scene staring at his map, equally startled by Harris's sudden appearance.*

American (*startled*): Yow! I thought I was in here alone. Can you read this thing?

> *Harris waves aside the map as being irrelevant.*

Harris: Follow me if you'd like. We're just going to go in for a couple of minutes, then turn around and come out again.

American: That's mighty kind. I've been stuck in here for almost an hour.

> *As they are about to leave, a Woman on the verge of tears enters from another direction with a baby in her arms.*

Woman: Oh, thank God! I'd given up all hope of ever seeing my family or my home again. Get me out of this wretched place!

> *The American points at Harris.*

American: That fella knows the way.

Harris: The only one with a cool head, it seems.

Woman: Let me take your arm. I don't want to lose you.

Harris: Pleasure.

> *Music. The five of them set off and the lights change for the 'Maze Wandering.' After a bit of wandering Harris and the American enter from one direction with no sign of the others.*

American *(to Harris)*: It's big, isn't it?

Harris: One of the largest in Europe.

> *Harris looks around attempting to get his bearings as George and Jerome and Montmorency enter from a different direction, equally disoriented, and startling Harris somewhat.*

American: It must be, because we've walked a good two miles already.

Harris: It does seem strange...

> *George crosses to look at a handkerchief lying on the ground. The Woman re-enters a moment later, a trifle frantic.*

George: We passed that handkerchief 10 minutes ago.

Harris *(looks at it):* Impossible.

> *He reaches out with his toe to nudge it as though it must be some kind of a mirage.*

Woman: No it isn't! That's my handkerchief! The baby dropped it. We're going around in circles!

> *An awkward silence as all turn and look at Harris, who retreats to his map.*

Harris: Let's have a gander at the old map.

American: The map's fine if you know whereabouts we are in it right now!

> *Baby cries. Montmorency howls. Jerome comforts him.*

Woman *(to the baby):* There, there. I feel the same way. We both wish we'd never laid eyes on him.

Harris *(head in the map):* I think I've got it now.

Woman: Super. When you've found the way out, send help. But I'm not walking another step with you.

> *She sits down on the bench defiantly. George*

timidly edges over to stand near her. Jerome then eases away from Harris and edges towards the relative safety of George and the Woman.

Harris: I can't help feeling that to a certain extent my popularity is waning.

American *(straightens his hat and braces)*: I'll chance it. Let's go.

Music. Harris and American wander off. A few moments later Harris re-enters alone, his head in his map.

Harris *(still in his map)*: That's got it!

Woman: Oh, well done you. In record time, too.

This startles Harris, who looks around him, then returns to his map. Unseen by Harris, the American re-enters from a different place, looking disoriented and angry.

Harris *(thoughtfully, examining the map)*: Maybe our best bet would be to go back to the entrance and start all over again...

The American crosses to Harris, grabs the map and crumples it, then stands threateningly glowering at him. The Woman takes a few steps forward and elbows her way in front of the American so that she might get first crack at him.

Harris suddenly makes a break for it. George and Jerome, startled, follow a moment later, realizing they're in danger. The American Man and the Woman follow after them in pursuit. Perhaps SFX mob voices.

Music as the lights crossfade.

Scene 10

When the lights restore, a table and chairs have been set in place to establish a pub. Jerome and George enter furtively. Jerome sits at a table that's been moved into place for them, while George remains on his feet somewhat anxious and breathless.

George: I think we lost them...

Jerome: If it wasn't for the baby, that woman would have snapped Harris in two like a twig.

George: I've never seen a woman in a bustle move that fast.

Harris runs on, winded and panting, and keeps glancing back to see if he's being followed.

Harris *(panting)*: Told you. Damn fine maze.

George: I'd say.

Harris *(panting)*: They must have moved those hedges since I was there last.

Jerome ignores Harris admires the atmosphere of the pub. Harris sits.

Jerome: Life has its pluses and its minuses, Harris. And your ability to find a pub while being chased by an angry mob is a definite plus.

A barmaid serves them pints of beer, then exits. George sits, still somewhat anxious.

Harris: Ingrates. There I was, reflecting on the beauty of nature and the brotherhood of man with a job lot of perfect strangers, and they do nothing but whinge

37

about handkerchiefs and maps! It makes me want to kill them and their family and all their friends and relations.

Jerome: Perhaps that's a bit strong.

Harris: Not a bit of it. Serve 'em all jolly well right. Then I'd burn down their houses and sing comic songs on the ruins.

George: I didn't know you sang!

Jerome *(quickly)*: George! Schtum…!

Harris: Just funny songs, you know. Once people have heard my patter, they simply can't… well, I remember once…

> *And he tells George a story or two about his accomplishments as Jerome talks to the audience.*

Jerome *(out)*: It is one of Harris's fixed ideas that he is an hilarious and spellbinding performer, just as it is the fixed idea of his friends that he *is* not, never will be, and ought not be allowed to try.

> *Barmaid enters and talks to the audience and the pub customers.*

Barmaid: 'Scuse me, if I could have your attention, ladies and gents. We have a distinguished guest from Germany, Mister Herr Schlossen Bossen, with us, and he's agreed to favour us with a ballad what's very popular in his country—

> *A German Singer – Herr Schlossen Bossen – enters the pub wearing lederhosen. He bows gravely.*

Barmaid: — So lend an ear and I'm sure we'll all become more cultivated as a result.

Herr Schlossen Bossen bows as Barmaid exits.

George: I've heard of him! He's supposed to be terrifically funny.

Harris: His clothes are certainly funny. What's he dressed for? Wrestling bears or something?

George *(sotto voce):*   He sings these hysterically funny songs, but because he's so serious about it and they're in German, you can't tell. *(beat)* At least, I think he's the one...

Harris: German? How the devil are we supposed to understand him?!

George *(sotto voce):*   Be polite and pretend you understand.

Harris: If it's German humour, I'll definitely be pretending.

> *George shushes Harris as Jerome talks to the audience. A recorded piano accompaniment starts.*
>
> *Jerome narrates throughout.*

Jerome *(out):*   George assured us that it was the funniest song that had ever been written, and it was this German chap's air of intense seriousness that made it that much more hilarious. Harris said if he didn't understand every single word, he would make a special effort to appear as though he did.

> *The music is very dour and dirge-like; a Schubert lieder, or something of that ilk. The German begins to 'sing.' [Soundlessly, as his voice is also recorded.] After a line or two, George laughs and nudges Harris, who barks out a mechanical "Ha*

Ha."

*The German is a trifle thrown but continues.
George tries again, pointedly laughing in Harris's
direction. Harris laughs with effort. Bossen
shoots them a look. George smiles back and
waves, nudging Harris to wave as well, which he
does. Harris and George continue to show their
appreciation, if utter lack of comprehension, of his
Teutonic humour.*

Jerome *(out)*: We later discovered that George had got it
completely wrong, and the man was, in fact, singing
an extremely tragic love song, with such jolly lyrics as,
"Love has proved false", "I am betrayed," and "Cease,
wretched heart, to beat."

*Harris and George continue to strain with
artificial laughter, believing that they are doing
foreign relationships a great turn.*

*The performance ends. The German walks over
to them, spits at their feet, then storms off. They
applaud.*

Jerome *(out)*: George and Harris did, however, answer the
question of how land wars get started.

Harris *(rising)*: All right, all right, I can feel all your eyes
imploring me —

Jerome *(frantic whisper)*:   — Harris! —

*He attempts to restrain Harris, but it is too late.
He talks to the audience.*

Harris: It's time we showed good old England has a sense of
humour too, and sang for our supper.

Harris clears his throat, perhaps gargles with some beer.

Jerome *(out):* It's one of Harris's tragic misconceptions that he can sing.

Harris: Everyone join in! It's that old tune... you know it...

> *He tunelessly attempts to hum a tune vaguely in the Gilbert & Sullivan style.*

Harris: The whatsitsname... with all the... You know the one...!

> *He claps his hands, stamps his foot, and various attempts to establish a tempo.*

> *SFX distant angry voices.*

Harris: And then you sing, "With a Ho Ho Ho" or some such nonsense, merry villagers and all that rubbish.

> *George sees danger approaching from offstage.*

George: It's the mob from the Maze...!

Harris: Right, from the top...! With a one, two, three...

Jerome: Harris!

> *SFX angry voices approaching from offstage.*

> *Jerome and George come up behind Harris, clasp a hand over his mouth, and cart him off as the lights fade to black.*

> *Music.*

Scene 11

When the lights restore, the men have settled themselves back in the boat and continue their journey upriver. Jerome rows wearily. Harris reclines and sings to himself cheerfully. George studies a map.

Harris: It's times like this I kick myself for not singing more often.

Jerome: Say the word and we'll kick you, too.

George *(looking at map)*: According to this, we should have reached Bell Weir lock a good time ago...

Jerome: Are you sure that map isn't someone's practical joke?

George *(looking at map)*: Magna Carta Island looks like a pretty part of the river…

Jerome: Well, I've got forty miles of river under my oars, and I don't want scenery. I want my dinner!.

He abandons the oars.

Harris: There, there, J. No need for melodrama.

Jerome: And I'm fed up with this bloody trip!

Harris: We'll tie up here and have something to eat.

> *Music. A silence falls as they bring the boat to the shore and disembark. Jerome starts unloading the boat. Harris grabs the food hamper and is about to eat something from it when George speaks up.*

George: We'd better get the tent up before it gets too dark while we can still see what we're doing.

Harris glowers at George.

Jerome: He's probably right, you know.

> *Harris puts back the food, and then over-aggressively begins hauling out the poles for the boat cover. As the pile grows, they consider this tangle of tubes and brackets and ropes with incomprehension.*

Harris: So, tell us, George. How does this work?

George: Well…

> *George unfolds a paper with the instructions. He turns it clockwise then counterclockwise a few times to try and make sense of it.*

George: It's… it's… At least I *think* it's…..

> *He looks at the pile of poles and such, attempting to relate what's on the picture to what's on the ground. He then hands this to Jerome.*

George: As best as I can remember, you fit the gigantic croquet hoops in little slots somewhere, attach the cross bars then stretch the canvas over the top, and fasten it down. Ten minutes work.

> *Jerome has been trying to make sense of the instructions. He hands Harris the instructions and wades into the fray, picking up one piece then another in the hope that it will suddenly all make sense. Harris stares at the instructions.*

Harris (*dubiously*): Ten minutes…

> *Music underscores this sequence. The men unfold the cover, and set about preparing it to*

be stretched over the hoops. This will never happen. The fabric should be something both light in weight and voluminous in size, so that what the audience sees is something like a very abstract modern dance of three figures completely enveloped in billowing fabric. Poles – sections of the hoops intended to support the cover – should be employed to contribute to the struggle that is apparently going on beneath.

As this sequence comes to an end, Harris has an encounter between one of the hoops and his head. An SFX 'clang' would not be out of place.

At the end of this tent-raising sequence – perhaps a minute in length – the result is that the three men surrender, exhausted, beside or beneath the folds of the fabric. In short, it never does come close to being erected over the boat.

When the lights fully restore, the cover is splayed shapelessly across the ground. Harris, having been soundly clipped across his head, is now having trouble with his ears, which are probably ringing. He shakes his head and rubs his ears in an attempt to get his hearing back. Jerome stretches his badly strained shoulder and arm. George crawls out from underneath the cover and painfully gets to his feet.

Jerome (*out*):   Ten minutes may have been an under-estimate. Frankly, it's a wonder that any of us are alive to tell the tale.

George limps to the hamper and sets up the stove and kettle. Jerome collapses and watches him.

George: I'll put on the kettle.

Harris examines his straw hat, which has had the crown pushed through and out.

Harris *(speaking too loudly):* One of those bars clipped me across the head when I wasn't looking! And who the devil is ringing those bells...?!

Harris shakes his head and attempts to 'pop' his ears to see if they are still functioning. George is watching the kettle, while Jerome, nursing his wounds, also stares at the kettle. Harris pulls out the sheet of instructions again, once again trying to make sense of it.

George *(sotto voce):* It'll never boil if we watch it.

Jerome *(sotto voce):* We should talk very loudly about how we don't really want tea. That might help.

George *(sotto voce):* Good idea…

Harris sees them talking but can't hear them. He rubs his ears again.

Harris *(speaking too loudly):* What are you saying…? I can't hear anything...

Jerome *(hisses at Harris):* Shut up…!

Jerome then speaks loudly for the benefit of the kettle.

Jerome: I don't want any tea; do you, George?

Harris *(speaking too loudly):* I've gone deaf...!

George *(to Harris, sotto voce):* Don't look at it.

Harris *(speaking too loudly):* The hoops broke my ears!

George *(sotto voce):*   Don't look at it…!

Harris *(speaking too loudly):* What?

Jerome *(sotto voce):*   The kettle…! It can hear us.

Harris *(speaking too loudly):* It's what…?

Jerome *(sotto voce):*   Act like you don't care.

Harris *(speaking too loudly):* I *don't* care!

> *George shushes Harris, who is baffled. He tries to*
> *not look at the kettle, but keeps stealing glances*
> *in case he's missing something important. George*
> *talks loudly and slowly so as to be clearly heard by*
> *the kettle.*

George: No, thanks, J; I don't like tea. Let's have lemonade
instead. Tea's so indigestible.

> *Then to Harris, sotto voce.*

George: Say something.

Harris: What?

George *(sotto voce):*To the kettle. Talk to it.

Harris: I'm not —

Jerome *(hissing):*Harris!

> *Harris has an intense inner struggle before he*
> *finally relents.*

Harris: No tea for me. Give me a beer. That's the stuff. Better
yet, a whisky. Better yet, several whiskies. And while
you're at it, why don't you take that kettle and —

Jerome interrupts so as not to offend the kettle.

Jerome: — How's the lemonade coming? That's what we want —

The kettle whistles. Harris stares at them both disbelievingly.

George: Tea's on!

The lights fade as the tea is made and cups passed round, and food is unpacked from the hamper.

Scene 12

The same scene. A short time has passed. It is evening. They've had something to eat and are at peace. A lantern has been lit and the men are relaxed and sprawled in a state of post-dining contentment.

Jerome: How good one feels when you're full. Satisfied and content, noble-minded and kindly hearted. Before supper, I was quarrelsome and ill tempered. Now the world is my friend.

George: Why can't we always be like this? Far away from the pandemonium of city life with its sins and temptations, doing good, and leading sober, peaceful lives.

Harris: Not completely sober.

George: A soberness of spirit.

Harris: Ah. *(beat)* People tell me that a clear conscience makes you happy and contented.

Jerome: Maybe so. *(beat)* But a full stomach does the job pretty well too —

Harris: — and it's a damned sight easier to get hold of.

George: Very true. Very true.

> *The lights continue to gradually fade to night.*

Scene 13

The same. It is now night.

Slowly the three men rise and move to bed down for the night in the boat. As Harris and George disappear under the canvas, the lantern illuminates Jerome as he talks to the audience. The hoops were never successfully installed, and so the cover was never hoisted over the boat as a cover. It's been left lying spread around on the ground and over boat. The men use it as a kind of group blanket and tent, making do with whatever is at hand to serve as their beds. Once Harris has made himself comfortable in the boat, his feet are left sticking out from beneath the canvas.

Jerome *(out)*:   And so the day ended. We settled in for the night as best we could. Harris's feet, being a size that never ought to be let inside a small boat, caused some difficulty at first. But we turned this to our advantage.

> *George spreads some cloths on Harris's outstretched feet, and then disappears beneath the canvas.*

Jerome *(out)*:   It was a glorious night. The moon had slipped away and left the quiet earth alone with her stars. The day had been so full of fret and care, and our hearts so full of evil and bitter thoughts, that the world seemed hard and wrong to us. Then night, like some great loving mother, gently laid her hand upon our fevered hearts and smiled, and we closed our eyes and went to sleep.

The lantern extinguishes and Jerome disappears under the cover. We hear river sounds, lapping water, wind rustling and other gentle sounds of the night; then this, too, fades. As the lights fade to black, the last sound we hear in the darkness is George's banjo being tentatively plunked followed by Montmorency's howling.

ACT TWO

Scene 1

It is morning. George emerges slowly from beneath the canvas, squinting into the morning sun and generally looking a little worse for wear. A moment or two later, Jerome emerges looking much the same. He winces in the morning's brightness.

George: Sun's up.

Jerome: That's putting it mildly.

Jerome tries to gauge the time by peering at the sun.

Jerome: Slept late, have we?

George: Not very. Ten past six.

George twists and turns in an attempt to unknot his cramped frame. A resulting SFX "crack," whether visual or audible, would not be out of place. George is clearly in physical discomfort as he slowly straightens up and sets about some morning routine. Jerome is no better.

Jerome *(out)*: Every morning for the past week we had been up with the sun. As a rule, I undress and put my head on the pillow, then somebody bangs at the door and says it's half-past eight. Then why is it that when there is no earthly necessity for getting up for at least another two hours, we were wide awake at the crack of dawn? If there'd been any reason why we had to get up and get dressed then and there, we would have dozed off while we were staring at our watches and slept till ten.

George responds as he continues to sort out things from the tangle of the canvas without looking up.

George: It's the natural cussedness of things.

Jerome *(out)*:   One does not yearn for "just another five minutes" lying on the floorboards of a boat with your suitcase for a pillow.

George clips Jerome across the side of the head with a tin pail. Jerome does not lash back, but accepts this as being par for the course. George picks up an oar to set it out of the way.

George: I hate to see Harris missing this holiday fun.

George jabs Harris with the oar.

Harris: Whaaaa...

George: We were wondering who was going in swimming first.

Harris looks groggily over the side of the boat.

Harris: Looks damp.

Harris slowly comes to life and look at the water, testing for temperature and moisture and such. He picks up the guidebook.

Jerome *(looking at the water with no enthusiasm)*:   It seemed like such a good idea to go for a dip first thing in the morning when we were back in the city. But the water looks so... different... when you see it in person.

Harris: Where are we?

George: Coming up to Abingdon.

Jerome *(still considering)*: The moment I strip down to my bathing drawers, an arctic wind is going to come sweeping in from the fjords. Happens every time. You watch.

George: Give you an appetite.

Harris: If going for a swim is going to make J eat more than he usually does, I'm against it.

George: Hear, hear.

Harris *(reading)*: Ever hear of a Mr. W. Lee?

Jerome: No.

Harris *(reading and gesturing vaguely)*: He's buried in the graveyard of St. Helen's Church over there somewhere. According to local history, "...he died in 1637 and had in his lifetime issue from his loins two hundred lacking but three."

George: Friendly fellow.

Jerome: Very.

Harris: Do the math, that's a hundred and ninety-seven offspring. Probably means he's one of our ancestors.

> *They exchange glances. Harris returns to the guidebook. Jerome continues to stare at the water as George continues to reload their stuff.*

Harris: If you're going in, grab us a couple of kippers for breakfast.

Jerome *(staring the water)*: I hate to disturb the fish. They're probably sleeping

Harris *(reads)*: Apparently there's excellent fishing nearby. "There is no spot in the world where you can fish for any longer period than at Abingdon."

George: You can fish until moss starts growing on you, but you won't catch anything in old Father Thames except minnows and old shoes.

Harris *(reads)*: "Trout and perch are to be found in abundance..."

George: Well, yes, when you're out for walks along the shore, trout and perch will swim up and stand half out of the water with their mouths open begging for snacks. And if you wade in, they crowd round your ankles and trip you up. But go after them with a bit of worm on the end of a hook? They aren't falling for that.

> *Harris takes one last look at the book, then tosses it into the river. SFX splash.*

Harris: Pub?

Jerome & George: Pub.

> *The lights crossfade.*

Scene 2

> *Later that day. When the lights restore, the men are in the boat. George rows. SFX of various*

rivers noises – engines, voices, et cetera – on a weekend afternoon.

Jerome *(out)*: It was just before the Henley Regatta, and we had endless close encounters with steam launches all morning. They were everywhere! I hate these power boats: every rowing man does. Whenever I see one, I have an irresistible urge to lure it to a lonely part of the river and shove its head under water. Makes you yearn for the good old days when you could tell people what you really thought of them with a bow and arrow, or a hatchet.

SFX steam whistle. Harris and George react to this, scouting around for the source.

Jerome *(out)*: They blow their damned horns and toot their whistles and expect you to clear out of the road. So we devised a strategy.

SFX steam whistle.

Harris: Steam launch coming...

The three quickly assume casual positions with their backs to the [unseen] launch.

Harris: Stand by...

SFX steam whistle. They begin their performance.

George: Did you hear something, J?

Jerome: Wind rustling through the trees...?

Harris looks left, then right, then finally behind him. He peers as though having difficulty seeing it.

Harris: What the...? J, look: it's some kind of boat...

SFX steam whistle and engine noises approaching.

Jerome and George look in every direction but the correct one. Then having spotted the now-angry boat, all wave and ad lib friendly "Hallos!"

They feign confusion about what to do, fumbling with oars, and getting themselves purposely entangled in rope. A cacophony of frantic SFX voices "Get out of the way!" and so forth are shouted from boats on the river, with repeated blasts of the steam launch's whistle.

The three men watch the launch pass, perhaps rocking in its wake.

Jerome, all sweetness and light, waves to the launch as it passes, and calls to the people onboard.

Jerome: Sorry! Sorry! *(beat)* Any chance of a tow...?

Long, angry SFX steam whistle, fading as it disappears down the river.

They lie back in their boat and enjoy the sun.

Harris: It really is the simple pleasures, isn't it.

The lights fade.

Scene 3

When the lights restore, George is rowing but is irritated at doing so. Harris dozes and snores, waking himself up doing so.

Jerome *(out)*: In a small boat, it's the fixed idea of each member of the crew that he is the one doing all the work.

> *George stops rowing, somewhat petulantly.*

George: I've never seen such a couple of lazy skulks as you two.

Harris: Fancy George talking about work. Why, a half-hour of it would kill him.

> *Harris closes his eyes and reclines as George begins to row again.*

Jerome *(out)*: Personally, I like work: it fascinates me. I can sit and look at it for hours. You cannot give me too much of it. My flat is so full of it now that there's hardly an inch of room for any more. Some of my work has been in my possession for years, with not a fingerprint on it.

George: Perhaps it's time you two did a bit for a change…!?

> *Neither of the other two take notice. Harris is yawning, and Jerome continues talking to the audience. Harris might start eating some pistachio nuts, which he cracks as he lounges and talks.*

Jerome: I take pride in my work. I take it down every now and then to dust it. To be perfectly frank, the idea of getting rid of it nearly breaks my heart.

Harris: I enjoy a hard day's work, too. But I like to be fair. I don't want to ask for more than my proper share.

> *George is grim. Jerome is amused at Harris's lack of insight.*

Jerome *(out)*: That's Harris all over – always ready to take the burden of everything himself and put it on the backs of other people.

George: I'm doing more than my fair share, I can tell you.

Harris *(surprised, he talks to J)*: Have you ever seen George really work before?

> *Jerome is busy packing his pipe, as George tosses down the oars again.*

George *(to Harris)*: Well, I don't see how you would know much about it…!

Harris: Now, George; temper —

George: You've been asleep half the time! *(to Jerome)* Have you ever seen him fully awake except at mealtimes?!

Jerome: Not really, but —

Harris: Well, hang it, I've done more than old J, anyhow!

Jerome: What…?!

George: You couldn't very well have done less…!

Harris: I suppose J thinks he's the passenger!!

> *Everyone is now angry at everyone. Harris sulks, George begins to row again, and Jerome fusses with his pipe. After a tense silence, Jerome talks to the audience.*

Jerome *(out)*: And this was their gratitude to me for having brought them and their wretched boat all the way up from Kingston. After having superintended and managed everything for them, taken care of them and slaved for them…

He shakes his head in dismay.

Jerome *(out)*: It's the way of the world.

The lights fade.

Scene 4

The men boat is tied up, and the three men are looking somewhat frayed around the edges. The days have begun to blur into one another. Harris begins to examine his jacket, with Jerome following in turn.

Harris: My jacket's filthy.

Jerome: Mine too.

Harris: It's like a map of the week's dinners.

Jerome: Got some of yesterday's breakfast over here.

Harris: There's fish on my lapel…

George chuckles at a classic joke he's remembered.

George: That reminds me of a funny story —

Jerome *(examining a spot)*: I can't tell what's pattern and what's fallout.

George: There were these two Italian policemen —

Harris *(rubbing his jacket)*: If you rub it in, it disappears.

George: — No, there were three of them —

Harris: No. Hold on, it just rubs it in —

George: — hold on, they weren't Italian; they were French, I think. Where's Tuscany, again?

Jerome: I've got stout —

Harris: Beer and whisky are here somewhere. (*to J*) Remember?

Jerome (*smiles*): Yes.

George: Anyway, they went to a monastery looking for… what was it…?

Jerome: — Cabbage and turnip —

George: — Doesn't matter. They went to this monastery… No, there were two of them —

Harris: I'm a walking garbage bin.

George: — And the first man said, "Hold on, isn't this a monastery?" —

Jerome: Time we wash our clothes before they start moving on their own.

George: — And the Mother Superior said —

Harris: That's the great thing about this fabric. Everything becomes part of the pattern…!

George: She said —

Jerome: Let's strip off our clothes and give them a rinse.

George (*confused*): What? No, she said… oh, never mind.

Jerome: George, you're the expert. How does this work?

George: What? Oh, simple. You soak the clothes in the river, rub the cloth against itself, rinse thoroughly, then hang them out to dry. Two minutes work.

Harris: Righto.

> *Harris and Jerome remove their trousers and set to work. George has given up on his joke, and pulls out his banjo and plunks away.*

Harris: Aren't you doing yours?

George: I'll wait 'til you two are finished. Don't want to tip the boat.

> *Harris dunks his trousers upstage of the boat – perhaps in an unseen bin of water – and washes them with great gusto.*

Jerome: How is it going?

> *Harris holds his trousers up to examine them.*

Harris: They're getting dirtier. J, you try it.

> *Jerome dunks his pants into the water. George plunks on his banjo as he watches them rubbing their clothing furiously.*

George: Maybe you're doing something wrong. Don't forget the elbow grease.

Harris: Are you sure this works...?

Jerome: — And how long do you have to rub...?

George: Well, I've never done it *myself* exactly.

Harris turns icy cold.

Harris: What...?

George: Dozens of people have told me about how simple it is.

Harris *(with menace):* Give me yours. Let's find out for certain.

George: Now that simply doesn't make sense. You've already tried it, and it clearly—

Harris *(with icy charm):* You can give them to me, or you can *wear* them in.

> *George quickly removes his trousers and hands them to Harris, then sits down again, never taking his eyes off of Harris. Harris takes the trousers, thrusts them into the water, splashes them around briefly, then pulls them out and tosses the sodden mess back into George's lap.*

Harris: Sorry, George. Still dirty.

Jerome: The river looks cleaner, anyhow. We'll have to head into town and have these things cleaned.

Harris: Wearing what?!

> *Music. They look at one another in their respective states of undress. Then Harris and George exit with the boat and their clothes as the lights fade.*

Scene 5

When the lights restore, Jerome talks to the audience in a village street scene.

Jerome *(out)*:   I'm all for nature, but I had become a little weary of having to carve out our niche in the wilderness every night. We decided to lay over in town for a few days, get our clothes properly cleaned, and have something to eat that didn't taste like wet socks or damp dog.

> *SFX bark.*

Jerome *(out)*:   Sorry, old boy.

> *Jerome comforts Montmorency as he talks out to the audience, and creating the sense of Montmorency being there among us.*

Jerome *(out)*:   Montmorency welcomed the change. He doesn't revel in romantic solitude. Give him something noisy, and if it's a bit ragged around the edges, so much the better. To look at him, you'd imagine he was a kind of angel sent upon the earth in the shape of a small fox terrier. He has a sort of "Oh what a wicked world" and "I'm thinking of Mother" expression that's brought tears to the eyes of pious old ladies.

> *SFX bark.*

Jerome *(out)*:   But after dragging him snarling and kicking out of a hundred and fourteen fights, and him bringing me a dead skunk for my inspection, I realized he was not quite the innocent he pretended to be. To acquire as many foul smells and get into as many scraps with other dogs and cats as possible: That is Montmorency's idea of 'Life.' Which is what he went in search of, happily trotting along with us into town for a few days. We found a washerwoman...

> *Harris and George have re-entered carrying bundles of clothes. A Washerwoman has entered from the opposite side and meets them. She looks at their bundle and sniffs suspiciously.*

Washerwoman: Do you want these buried or burned?

George: They just need a rinsing to get the river water out of
them.

Washerwoman: More in the nature of excavating, if you ask
me.

> *She sniffs the clothes and looks them over.*

Harris: Pay her, George.

Washerwoman: I'll only charge you triple because you seem
like nice boys.

Harris: Pay her, George.

> *He does. They try to hand her the bundles.*

Washerwoman: I'm not touching that lot without gloves. This
way.

> *Harris and George exit following the woman and
> the lights change.*

Jerome *(out)*: At that moment, a cat appeared in front of us and
began to amble across the road. Montmorency gave a
cry of joy – a kind of "Christmas came early!" yelp of
delight – and flew after his prey.

> *Jerome's eyes follow the unseen Montmorency
> and the Cat as he narrates the action.*

Jerome *(out)*: I have never seen a larger nor a more
disreputable-looking cat. He was a black Tom that had
lost half its tail, one of its ears, and a fairly appreciable
proportion of its nose. He sauntered down the High
Street with a calm, contented air as Montmorency bore
down on him at about forty miles per hour. The feckless

creature didn't grasp that his life was all but over as he sat himself down in the middle of the road and gave Montmorency the Stink Eye. That startled Monty, and made him stop dead in his tracks. The cat yawned, then gave him a blank look that seemed to say, "Yes? You want something?"

Jerome has been watching the unseen Montmorency with the Cat.

Jerome *(out)*: Montmorency does not lack pluck. But there was something about the look of that cat that would have chilled the heart of the boldest dog. Neither spoke; but the conversation I imagined went something like this.

Jerome voices Montmorency, with a Scots accent. The Actor has ambled on, cigarette in hand, to voice the Cat. The Actor perhaps wears a black patch over one eye to suggest a rough and ready soul, with an accent to match. He stands nearby Jerome, although unnoticed as of yet. They do nothing to suggest "dog" or "cat"; they simply convey the thoughts and emotions.

Jerome as Montmorency turns and is startled to see the Cat there.

Cat: Can I help you?

Montmorency: What...? Oh, no... no, thanks.

Cat: Speak up if there's sumfing you wants.

Montmorency *(backing away)*: Oh, no - nothing at all. I – I'm afraid I made a mistake. Thought I knew you. Very embarrassing. Awfully sorry to disturb you.

Cat: Sure there's nuffing else?

Montmorency (*backing away*): No, not a thing. Very kind of you. 'Morning.

Cat: 'Mornin'.

> *Jerome resumes being Jerome as the Actor exits.*

Jerome (*out*): Then the cat rose and went on his way. Montmorency, fitting what he calls his tail carefully into its groove, came back to us and took up a position at the rear of our small group. To this day, if you say the word "Cat" to Montmorency, he will visibly flinch and look piteously at you, as if to say, "Please. Don't."

> *The lights start to fade.*

Jerome (*out*): Three days later we had bathed, had clean clothes, and were back in our boat, and we headed north towards Reading.

> *In the background, Harris and George re-enter carrying their trousers. They climb in to them, and bring Jerome his trousers, and he climbs into his.*
>
> *The lights fade.*

Scene 6

> *When the lights restore, the men are on the bank of the river setting out things for lunch. Jerome talks to the audience.*

Jerome (*out*): Two or three hundred years ago, Reading was a popular place to dash off to when things got unpleasant in London. Parliament escaped here whenever a plague rolled through town, and in 1625 the lawyers followed suit. It must have been worthwhile having a dash of plague now and again to flush out both the lawyers *and* the politicians.

Harris: I think we could all use a cup of tea. George, see if you can't find some water.

> *Jerome and Harris set to work laying out food from the hamper, and the stove for tea. George, kettle in hand, begins to go in search of water as a decrepit Old Man enters. He speaks with a West Country accent.*

George: Hello...!

Old Man: How do.

George: This your land?

Old Man: Far as you can see. From beyond them cows to —

George: Yes, yes, super. Look, I was wondering if could you spare us a little water?

Old Man: Certainly. Take as much as you want and leave the rest.

George: Thank you so much. *(He looks about)* Where... where do you keep it?

Old Man: Always been in the same place, my boy. Just behind you.

George: I don't see it.

Old Man: They ain't moved it, have they? Why, bless me, where's your eyes? There's enough of it to see, ain't there?

He turns George around and points him towards the river.

George: Oh. Right. But we can't drink the river, you know.

Old Man: No. *(beat)* But you can drink some of it. Take what you like and leave the rest.

> *He takes George's arm and leads him to the river, saying something that we can't hear, pats him paternally on the back and then exits.*
>
> *George considers the water carefully, then reluctantly fills the kettle and returns to the others, still warily eyeing the water in his kettle.*

George: He said it's what he's drunk for the last 15 year, and *(George echoes the man's accent)* '…it ne'er done him no harm.'

Harris: Doesn't look like it did him much good either, if you ask me.

> *They each take a turn looking at the water in the kettle, sniffing and peering at it.*

Jerome: What the eye does not see, the stomach does not get upset over.

Harris: If we boil it, it should be all right. Get rid of the invisible creepy crawlies.

> *The kettle is put on the fire, and tea put in to it as George serves up some sandwiches.*

George: What we need is something to eat. Bread. Bit of butter… there you are, J. Harris, plenty of beef…. and one for me.

Harris: Pass the mustard, George.

George: Where is it?

Jerome: Bottom of the hamper, I think.

Harris: You can work up a really exceptional appetite doing more than your fair share of work. What about that mustard?

> *George is now hunting desperately for the mustard.*

George: Where is it?

Harris: There's no mustard...?

Jerome: No mustard...!?

George: That's what I'm saying!!

Jerome: I don't believe I have ever in my life wanted mustard as badly as I do right now.

Harris: It's got to be there!

> *There is a long, tense silence. Harris rummages through the hamper for the mustard without success. George looks at his sandwich sourly.*

George: I'd give *anything* for a bit of mustard right now.

Harris: It's not there. Not a spoonful.

> *They slump down and chew in mournful silence. After a moment, George gives the tea a resigned stir.*

George: Tea's up.

> *Harris and Jerome set out cups and saucers.*
> *George pours and cups are passed round. Each*
> *gives his cup a careful examination.*

George: Looks all right.

Harris: Smells respectable.

Jerome I needed this.

> *He takes a tentative first sip, which passes muster;*
> *then drinks the rest of the cup down in one gulp.*
> *The others watch and wait for an 'All Clear.'*

Jerome *(out)*: Wonderful.

> *Something catches George's attention on the*
> *water.*

George: What's that?

Jerome & Harris: What's what?

George: That…!

> *He points. All eyes follow an object as it floats*
> *past. Jerome talks to the audience, while Harris*
> *and George remained fixated on the water.*

Jerome *(out)*: Harris and I followed his gaze and saw coming
towards us, on the sluggish current a… a…

Harris: It's a dog…

Jerome *(out)*: It was one of the quietest and peaceful-est
dogs I have ever seen. I never met a dog who seemed
more contented and less contentious. He was floating
dreamily on his back, his four legs stuck up straight into
the air.

George: Looks dead to me.

Jerome *(out)*: It was what I'd call a full-bodied dog with a well-developed chest. On he came, serene, dignified, and calm, until he was abreast of our boat, and there, among the rushes, he eased up, and settled down cozily for the evening.

George: Don't think I'll have any after all.

George empties his cup out.

Harris *(following suit)*: I'm not too thirsty myself. Top you up, J?

Jerome stares into his cup.

Jerome: No, thank you. Um… do you think I'll get Typhoid?

George: Oh, don't be stupid! I think you have a very good chance of avoiding it. Anyhow, you'll know in a week or so.

Harris: You'll probably try and catch it just to avoid work. Bit of dog-flavoured tea probably do you a world of good.

Harris and George chuckle. Jerome frets. George lies back to relax, while Harris, rooting around, discovers a happy surprise in the bottom of the hamper.

Harris: Hallo. Bit of bright news…

Jerome: What now? Is the boat on fire?

Harris: Pineapple for dessert…!

He holds up a tin in triumph then passes it to George and Jerome.

George: Pineapple!

> *They examine the tin appreciatively, sniffing it and measuring the weight of its promise. Jerome starts to brighten up.*

Harris: Tinned pineapple. Nothing quite like it. Much better than the real thing.

Jerome: It's the sauce they pack it in. It's like liquid sunshine. Not too sweet —

Harris: — and the fruit is so crisp and fresh. An apple has nothing on it.

Jerome: Or a pear.

Harris: A pear!? Hah! You might as well have said "gooseberries," or "banana!"

> *George has continued to search through the hamper and other baskets.*

George: Where's the opener?

Harris: The what?

George: The opener. Where's the tin opener?

> *Beat.*

Harris: I don't have any opener.

George: J?

Jerome: I know we packed one. I'm sure we did. At least I think —

Harris: — A knife might work.

71

George: I have a spoon.

Harris: Knife, George. Knife! Read my lips. Here, pass the tin over.

> *Harris takes out a knife and takes two or three tentative stabs at it, then really lets go, only managing to gore himself.*

Harris: Aaaaggg-gggg-gggg!!

George: I'll have a go at it with these.

> *George picks up some scissors and has a go.*

George: Yaaaaahhhhhhh!!!!

Jerome: I'll get it open.

> *He picks up an oar and begins hammering the tin, tentatively at first, but eventually escalating into thrashing and smashing, but making no progress in opening the tin. He shrieks in a fury, and then all three attack it wildly, hammering and jumping on it with various curses and oaths.*
>
> *They eventually stop, panting for breath. Harris, winded and enraged, grabs the tin and holds it up for them to see.*

Harris: Look at it! The tin! It's bent into sort of a demented smile. The damned thing's grinning at us! You bastard!!

> *He hurls it offstage, then stands back, winded but triumphant. They quickly dump their things back into the boat. Harris then climbs in and shouts to the others.*

Harris: Now row!

And they row the boat away, Harris panting from exertion and staring grimly in the direction of where the tin disappeared under the water.

Harris: It'll never find us now...!

Music as the lights fade.

Scene 7

When the lights restore, the three men are back in the boat, with Harris at the oars, but not rowing. George is looking at something in the distance.

Jerome: What's the plan then?

Harris: Can't we just drift along for a bit? I've had my fill of pulling and pushing this scow up river.

Jerome: If we're going to make Oxford by Saturday, we've got to—

George has become very still, and gazes up at the sky.

Jerome *(to Harris)*: What's the matter with George?

Harris: You'll have to be more specific. *(to George)* George, J wants to know...

George puts his finger to his lips for silence.

George *(carefully)*: By some gross oversight on the part of nature... the wind seems to be blowing in the right direction for a change.

Music.

George moistens a finger and inserts it into the wind to check the velocity and direction, then nods in the affirmative. This buoys everyone's spirits.

If not the real thing, then the impression of a mast and sail being raised should be conveyed. Harris and Jerome settle into comfortable positions with blissful expressions, while George takes the tiller.

Jerome talks to the audience.

Jerome *(out)*: We put up our sail and all but flew across the water. There is no more thrilling sensation I know of than sailing. It comes as near to flying as man has got to yet, except in dreams. We were one with nature. No one spoke as we skimmed along the river, feeling like knights of some old legend, transported across a mystic lake into the unknown realm of twilight.

Beat.

Jerome *(out)*: But we did not go into the realm of twilight. Our sail blocked the view and we went bang into a fishing punt moored midstream.

SFX of a splintering crash, and the underscoring music stops abruptly. Jerome, Harris and George lurch forward accordingly. A Man and Woman stumble onstage as though thrown by force, clutching their fishing poles.

Woman *(simultaneous with Man)*: What in the blue blazes do you think you're doing?!

Man *(simultaneous with Woman)*: They're drunk. Or mad!

Woman: Or both!!

Harris: You ought to be grateful for a little excitement, sitting there fishing all day.

> *The Woman and Man are startled into silence for a moment, but only for a moment, by Harris's defiance. George attempts to ward him off.*

George: Harris...

Jerome *(out)*:   Harris has a gift for the undiplomatic.

> *The Man and Woman then lace into Harris, albeit soundlessly from the audience's point of view, but illustrated with many gestures. George winces and Jerome narrates to the audience.*

Jerome *(out)*:   They cursed us: not with any common cursory curse, but with long, carefully thought out comprehensive curses that embraced the whole of our careers, and went away into the distant future, and included all of our relations and everything connected with us. Really good, substantial curses.

> *Man and Woman exit. Harris shouts after them.*

Harris: I, for one, am shocked and truly grieved to hear persons of your advanced age give way to temper so fearfully.

> *Harris is hit with a bucket of water and fish – or something representing these. The lights fade and Harris tips his cap in their direction.*

Harris: 'Evening.

> *Harris slowly begins to tidy himself up.*

> *They transition the boat to the shore for supper.*

Jerome: And now what are we supposed to do for supper? Everything in the hamper's cold and wet with bits of fish everywhere.

There is a thoughtful if weary silence.

George: I know what might make us feel better.

Jerome & Harris: Not your banjo…!

George: No, no, no. An Irish stew! It's a good, hearty dish that'll soak up all those dreadful things you swallowed in your Dead Dog tea.

Harris: What's in it?

George: Whatever's left in the hamper, we chuck in. And if J keels over from his dead dog tea, we'll bung him in, too.

George grabs a pot.

Harris: What should we do?

George: Peel… oh, a dozen or so potatoes. I'll get things started.

He tosses Harris a bag of potatoes.

Harris (*baffled, examining a potato):* How are you supposed to —

George: Right. Now let's see what else we have….

Music.

George examines the contents of the hamper, continuously tossing things from the hamper into the pot.

Jerome and Harris get knives and begin to peel

potatoes, something they have never done before.
The peeling slowly consumes them.

George: Eggs, tin of salmon, cabbage… what's this?

George holds up something unrecognizable.

Jerome: Never saw it before in my life.

George: In it goes.

Harris and Jerome continue their peeling. As
they work and talk, some flying creature swarms
around George's head. He finally manages to kill
it after a struggle, and then adds it to the stew.
He continues searching around the perimeter, and
adding to the pot. Harris and Jerome continue to
talk and peel throughout this.

Harris: You know, I've never really looked at one of these
before. They're the most extraordinary damn things, all
bumps and warts and molehills.

Jerome: I saw a plaque in a church the other day. An elderly
lady in the parish bequeathed one pound a year to any
little boy or girl who had never been disrespectful to
their parents, never swore or told lies, and had never
been known to steal or to break windows.

Harris: Give all that up for a pound a year?

Jerome: Mmmm-hmmm.

Harris: Not worth it.

Harris: Where's George got to?

Jerome: Off collecting toadstools and eye of newt, I expect.

Harris: Quick.

> *Harris, joined by Jerome, gathers up all the detritus of their work, including the peelings, and chucks it all into the pot. George re-enters with both hands full of something, which he drops into the pot, resulting in an eruption of steam and perhaps an SFX.*

George: That should do it.

> *SFX bark. Harris sees Montmorency coming.*

Harris: Montmorency's brought something as well.

> *Montmorency's contribution is dropped on the ground in front of them.*

George: It's a rat.

Jerome: Looks dead.

Harris: Is he being ironic?

Jerome: Hard to know. Sometimes you can tell by his eyes...

> *Jerome and Harris both look carefully at Montmorency's eyes – or at least where we imagine Montmorency's eyes to be – to determine just how ironic he is being.*

George: Might be all right mixed up with the other stuff.

Jerome: I've never heard of water rats in Irish stew before.

Harris: If you never try a new thing, how can you tell what it's like? It's people like you that hamper the world's progress. Think of the man who first tried German sausages.

Jerome: Even so, I believe I've had my fill of animal-flavoured food and drink.

George: Well, here goes.

They all have a taste.

Jerome: It's… *(beat)* … well, unlike anything I've ever tasted before.

Harris: It's actually pretty good.

George: It is…!

Jerome: But I can't think how you'd describe it…

Harris: It's like… chocolate meringue lemon upside down cabbage roll potluck with potatoes, and a soupçon of… *(tries to think of the right word)*

George *(considering)*: Kerosene.

They nod in the affirmative and murmur happy agreement as they eat heartily.

Music as the lights fade.

Scene 8

When the lights restore, Jerome is rowing as though in a trance, while the other two look sourly at him.

Harris: Look at J, just sitting there, 'rowing.'

George: Makes you wonder why we chose to spend our vacation on the river in the first place.

Harris: Yes, why was that, again?

He considers the silent Jerome, who is making him uneasy. Harris directs his comment to George.

Harris: He's gone very quiet.

George: Perhaps he's sleep-rowing.

Harris: His eyes are open.

George: Doesn't mean a thing. I heard about this man who…

Jerome gently stops rowing and sets the oars at rest. This alarms George and Harris. They wait for him to explain himself. When he talks, he does so in an other-worldly manner.

Jerome: This world is only a probation, and man was born to trouble as the sparks fly upward.

George: It's what?

Jerome: I remember going swimming near Boulogne years ago. Not far from the beach, I was suddenly seized from behind by the neck, and forcibly plunged under water. I struggled violently, but whoever had hold of me was a perfect Hercules in strength, and any attempt to escape was hopeless. I gave up kicking and resigned myself to my fate.

He turns to talk to George, catching him off-guard and startling him.

Jerome: Fate's a funny thing, isn't it, George.

George: What? Oh, yes, yes…

Jerome: Then my captor's hands released me. I struggled to the surface, looking for this would-be murderer. He was standing a couple of feet away, laughing heartily. But then he caught sight of my face. He looked very startled and uneasy, then stammered, "I… I beg your pardon, I thought you were a friend of mine…"

Harris: Lucky he didn't mistake you for a relative, or he probably would have drowned you outright!

> *He chuckles. George is too nervous to join in. Jerome turns and looks at Harris with no discernable reaction, unnerving Harris.*

Harris *(to J)*: I mean to say, I hope you tore a strip off of him…

> *Jerome continues to be a blank canvas.*

George: I, uh… J? Are you….

> *Jerome is very thoughtful and serious, but likely hasn't heard a word anyone said. Finally…*

Jerome: I don't know about you men, but I don't want to be sinful and wicked anymore.

Harris: You what…?

Jerome: I could live in this little corner of the world. Look at that grey church wrapped with ivy, George! And those thatched roof cottages and those trees. *Trees*, Harris!

Harris: What about the trees…?

Jerome: This is the place where I want to spend the rest of my days, and never do any more wrong, and lead a blameless, beautiful life.

> *Peaceful music begins under. Harris and George listen in silence as Jerome extemporizes.*

81

Jerome: I'll forgive all my friends and relations – even the two of you – for your wickedness and cussedness, and I will bless you all.

Harris: Steady on, old man…

George *(sotto voce to Harris)*: What's he on about?

Harris *(sotto voce)*: He's slipped a gear. Don't make any sudden moves or they won't find our bodies for weeks.

Jerome: We're almost there…

George: Almost where?

Harris *(sotto voce)*: Just let him row.

> *A silence with music, everyone in the boat looking grim.*

> *The lights crossfade.*

Scene 9

> *When the lights restore, Jerome has returned to relative normalcy. No one is rowing as they are being given a tow. Despite this, they look exhausted and drained.*

Jerome *(out)*: The next morning, we met up with some friends at Reading Lock who had a steam launch, and they gave us a tow. It's wonderful being towed by a launch. To be honest, I prefer it to rowing. And it would have been more delightful still if there hadn't so many wretched small boats continually getting in our way. Something ought to be done about those nuisances. Something forceful.

SFX steam whistle. Jerome shouts at an unseen foe.

Jerome: That's right! I'm talking to YOU! Get out of the way! If I had my way, we'd run you and your little boat down just to teach you a lesson!

SFX steam whistle.

Jerome *(out)*: But once the launch cast us loose, our boat seemed to grow even smaller, as did our enthusiasm for the river.

The lights shift to suggest a small passage of time, and a distinct downturn in the atmosphere.

Jerome *(out)*: Harris wanted to make out that it was my turn to pull. This seemed to me most unreasonable. It had been arranged in the morning that I should bring the boat up to three miles above Reading. Well, here we were, thanks to my friends towing us, we were *ten* miles above Reading! Which clearly meant it was George and Harris's turn again. But I couldn't get them to see things in their proper light; so, to save argument, I took the sculls. Again.

Music. The lights crossfade.

Scene 10

The same. Time has passed. Jerome doles out portions of a meat pie that they have set aside for supper, which Harris and George take with no enthusiasm.

Harris: What do you call this?

83

Jerome: Supper.

Harris: It's damp. And clammy.

Jerome: *Everything* is damp and clammy.

> *George holds up a sodden lump of his pie.*

George: Cold veal pie? I thought we'd finally got rid of that. I'll pass.

> *He hands it back, and looks for something else from the hamper.*

Jerome: I know what I want. Rare roast beef, with crackling and Yorkshire pudding.

Harris: Wouldn't some Sole Béarnaise with those little potatoes be absolutely…

George: Could we please not discuss béarnaise sauce or anything hot until I manage to swallow my cold boiled mutton with no mustard? Would that be too much to ask?

> *A silence falls.*

Jerome *(out)*: Harris tried to feed the remains of his veal pie to Montmorency. But Monty took offence….

> *SFX mournful dog howl.*

Jerome *(out)*: …turned up his nose, then went and sat at the far end of the boat.

> *George shuffles cards.*

George: I'll give you a chance to win back what you've lost. Tuppence apiece, if memory serves.

Harris: Gambling breeds an unhealthy excitement when carried too far. Especially when I lose

> *Harris snatches the deck of cards and stuffs them into a pocket.*

Jerome *(out)*: It was not a merry evening.

> *The lights fade.*

Scene 11

> *The lights tighten in on Jerome as he talks to the audience.*

Jerome *(out)*: After that, a cloud seemed to descend over us and the boat. We were determined to make the last leg up to Oxford the next day. Harris was at the sculls and I was navigating. George noticed a cluster of people on the riverbank. We rowed over to see what had drawn them. As we got close, George blanched and drew back. It was the dead body of a woman. She lay lightly on the water, and her face was sweet and calm. It was not a beautiful face; it was too prematurely aged-looking, too thin and drawn, to be that. But it was a gentle, lovable face, in spite of its stamp of pinch and poverty. And on it was that look of restful peace that comes to the faces of the sick sometimes when at last the pain has left them.

> *The lights remain tight on Jerome as he talks, slowing beginning to dim.*

Jerome *(out)*: We found out the woman's story afterwards. It was an old, sad story. She had loved and had been deceived, or maybe she'd deceived herself. She'd had a child, her family had turned against her, and the man had left. Finally, when her frail child had passed away from its weak heart, her heart, too, just gave out. She'd come to this village, lay down in the cold water and the river had silenced her the pain. God help her.

Music as the lights dip to black.

Scene 12

Harris is wrestling with the oars, and George is attempting to find a comfortable position to huddle in and possibly sleep. Jerome talks to the audience.

Jerome *(out)*: We were up early the next morning. And the next. And the next after that. The boat seemed to change size and shape almost hourly.

Harris: Someone has sabotaged these oars. I'm not pointing any fingers, George, but...

George: Me! You were up sleepwalking half the night drinking hot toddys, and shouting about your umbrella being attacked by swans.

Harris: That was the whisky talking! And since you mention it, where is my umbrella?

> *George thrusts it at him. Harris opens it, and it is in tatters, and perhaps a few feathers flutter out. Harris tries to remember what happened.*
>
> *Montmorency howls. There is a tense silence.*

Jerome *(out)*: After a week on the river, little mishaps that you'd hardly notice on dry land drive you homicidal on the water. When Harris or George makes an ass of himself on dry land, I smile indulgently. When they behave in a chuckle-headed way on the river, I use the most blood-curdling language with them. Or when another boat gets in the way, I want to take an oar and kill all the people in it.

George: It might do us well to remember what Aristotle said…

Harris: Aristotle didn't have to sleep on the floor of a wet boat! And if I have to swallow one more piece of sodden bread and jam I'm going to… to… to… to…

> *SFX crack of thunder, a flash of lightning, which cuts Harris's fulminations short. All three look up to the heavens.*

Jerome *(out)*: And then it began to rain.

> *SFX rain and thunder as the lights fade to a stormy night.*

Scene 13

> *The same. SFX rain and thunder. Lightning flashes throughout. A lantern is lit. Jerome and George open and hide beneath umbrellas.*

Harris: Ha! Look at you, crouched 'neath brollys. It's just water. Do you some good! A Gypsy's life for me, unaffected by the whims of nature.

> *SFX thunder crack. Harris pulls up the collar of his coat.*

Jerome: Do you think it will stop by tonight?

George: Bound to stop. Bound to. *(beat)* Eventually.

Harris: We'll make some hot toddies…

SFX thunder and rain.

Harris: And before you know it —

Jerome: — We'll be dead.

SFX rain. They listen for a few moments. Then…

George: I had a friend who came up river two years ago. He slept out in a damp boat like this, on a night like this. He died in agony ten days later.

Beat.

Jerome: It would be awkward if one of us came down with something, miles from a doctor.

SFX thunder and lightning.

Harris: I had a friend who slept out in a tent on a night like this. Woke up in the morning a cripple for life. I'll introduce you to him if we make if back to town. He'll make your hearts bleed.

SFX thunder and lightning.

Jerome: George, pull out that banjo of yours and give us a song.

George takes out his banjo. After a moment or two of plucking and tuning, He plays and sings. Slowly, they all join in.

George *(singing)*:

*"In Scarlet town where I was born
There was a fair maid dwelling*

And every youth cried well away
For her name was Barbara Allen
'T'was in the merry month of May
The green buds were a swelling
Sweet William on his deathbed lay
For the love of Barbara Allen

Slowly slowly she got up
And slowly she came nigh him
And the only words to him she said
Young man I think you're..."

> *They have all joined in. At some point in the song, Montmorency howls and Harris and Jerome break into muffled sobs and choked voices. Harris eventually trails off, and then Jerome. George playing grinds to a halt, and he finally puts the banjo away.*

Harris: It's only two days more and we're young and strong. We may get over it all right.

George: There's always a chance.

> *SFX thunder and lightning.*

Jerome: As delightful as this is, the Alhambra would almost be livelier.

> *Harris wipes the water from his face and hair.*

Harris: They'd be serving dinner about now. Pity we made up our minds to stick to the boat.

> *SFX thunder and lightning.*

George: If we hadn't made up our minds to contract our certain deaths in this floating coffin, it might be worth mentioning that there's a train leaving in about an hour that would land us back in town in time for drink at the club.

A flash of lightning. Guilty looks are exchanged amongst them. Music.

Finally the lantern is extinguished, and in the silhouette of lightning flashes, we see the three men dragging the boat offstage as discreetly as they can manage.

Scene 14

As the lights restore, lightning continues to flash in the background and thunder can still be heard. We are now in a small cozy dining room. A Waiter carries on a small table and three chairs. Jerome, Harris and George enter and sit at a linen-covered table with china enjoying cigars and brandy. There is another crack of thunder and flash of lightning, and we see a Woman "outside" walk past the restaurant's window, struggling against the wind and the driving rain, being tosses about by the wind catching her umbrella. This comic ballet could last a minute or so, with the men silently enjoying the entertainment value. Finally she is swept out of view, and the men return their attention to the coziness of their little restaurant.

Harris: Well. We had a pleasant trip, and my hearty thanks to old Father Thames. But I think we did well to chuck it when we did.

George: Nature's all right and all the rest of it. But there's a great deal to be said in favour of a comfortable chair and a good cigar.

They toast.

Jerome Here's to three men well out of their boat!

> *Ad lib "Hear, hear", and glasses are 'clinked' in a toast. Montmorency barks, and Jerome pats his head.*

> *Jerome leaves the table and comes forward to speak out, cigar and brandy snifter in hand.*

Jerome *(out)*: We'd had exercise and fresh air and a change of scenery. We'd ripened the fruits of friendship. And while another week in that skiff might have jeopardized Harris' mental stability or George's well being at the hands of Harris's mental stability, our friendship had never been stronger.

> *Harris and George have left the table and moved centre-stage. Music begins – "Put on Your Tat-Ta's Little Girlie."*

Jerome *(out)*: And besides which, the amateur theatre season was still in full swing, and we had to practice our routine for the club show.

> *The Alhambra drop is unfurled once again.*

Harris: Now follow me...

> *As before, a routine is performed with individually characteristic interpretations and variations – but perhaps with a shade more coordination and skill. The Music continues, as does the routine. This time they sing the words to a single verse of "Put on Your Tat-Ta's Little Girlie", and dance. At the conclusion, the lights snap to black. And the play is over.*

Appendix

Guidebook Text

These are two pieces of text that Harris can use when reading from his guidebook:

Harris *(reading):* Saxon kings and Saxon revelry were buried side by side and Kingston's greatness passed away for a time, to rise once more when Hampton Court became the palace of the Tudors and the Stuarts, and the royal barges strained at their moorings on the river's bank, and bright-cloaked gallants swaggered down the water-steps to cry: 'What Ferry, ho! Gadzooks, gramercy.' The coronation feast had been something. Maybe boar's head stuffed with sugar-plums – sounds like a recipe for indigestion, if you ask me – and endless gallons of sack and mead…

Harris *(reading):* Many of the old houses speak very plainly of those days when Kingston was a royal borough. The large and spacious houses, with their oriel, latticed windows, their huge fireplaces, and their gabled roofs, breathe of the days of hose and doublet, of pearl-embroidered stomachers, and complicated oaths…

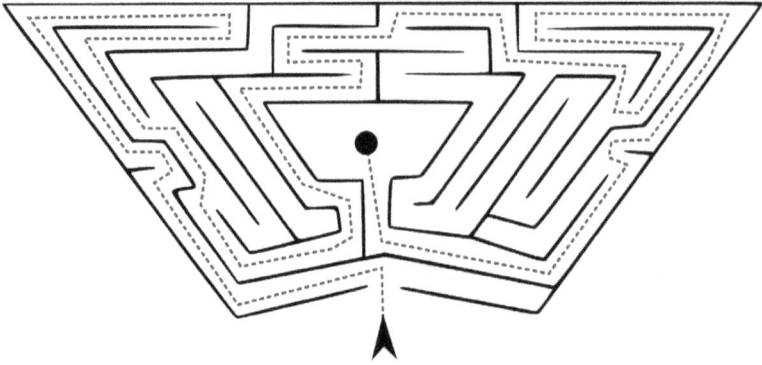

Hampton Court Maze

About the Author

Blake Heathcote worked as a freelance director and playwright, directing several Canadian premieres and more than a hundred other productions across Canada and in the United States. He was Artistic Director of the Showboat Festival Theatre for ten seasons, and founded Theatre in Port, both in Ontario, Canada.

He was assistant director to renowned Broadway director Hal Prince on three musicals, and worked with Sir Alan Ayckbourn in Scarborough, North Yorkshire, where Alan directed two of Blake's plays at the Stephen Joseph Theatre-in-the-Round.

Blake has written fifteen plays, including *Revenge of the Woman Dressed Largely in Black, Dressed to Kill, Roundabout,* and the adaptations *The Misanthrope, Christmas Carol: A Theatrical Storytelling, The Canterville Ghost,* and *Scapin.*

He has also written two television documentaries, and four non-fiction books: *Testaments of Honour, A Soldier's View, The Survivor,* and *Unremarkable: A Good Place to Start.*

JEROME K. JEROME

Jerome Klapka Jerome, author of 'Three Men in a Boat', one of the great comic masterpieces of the English language, was born in Walsall, Staffordshire, on 2nd May 1859, the youngest of four children. He left school at fourteen and worked variously as a clerk, a hack journalist, an actor ('I have played every part in Hamlet except Ophelia') and a schoolmaster. His first book 'On the Stage and Off' was published in 1885 and this was followed by numerous plays, books and magazine articles.

Jerome sat down to write Three Men in a Boat as soon as he returned from his honeymoon. The book, published in 1889, became an instant success and is still in print. Its popularity was such that the number of registered Thames boats went up fifty percent in the year following its publication, and it contributed significantly to the Thames becoming a tourist attraction. In its first twenty years alone, the book sold over a million copies worldwide. He died in 1927.

www.ingramcontent.com/pod-product-compliance
Lightning Source LLC
Chambersburg PA
CBHW062008040426
42447CB00010B/1972